Herb Kraus

# Accordion
## Basics

 Voggenreiter

C000114670

Layout: B & O

Translated by: Sylkie Monoff

Accordeon played by: Andrea Dünker

© 2013 Voggenreiter Verlag OHG
Viktoriastraße 25, 53173 Bonn/Germany
www.voggenreiter.de
Phone: 0228.93 575-0


ISBN: 978-3-8024-0953-0

# Preface

Welcome and thank you for buying *Accordion Basics*. This tutorial is your easy introduction to the world of accordion playing. In compiling *Accordion Basics* a special emphasis has been placed on easily understandable content and explanations.

Last but not least, the pedagogic and didactic experience of the author accounts for laying an optimal foundation for learning to play the piano – suited for teaching at music schools as well as the self-taught player.

No previous musical knowledge is required to start working with this book. All exercises have been developed to immediately allow you to play along and are arranged in ascending difficulty.

The exercises, songs and solo pieces are recorded on the included audio CD. The tracks are recorded in stereo so that you can increase or decrease the volume for the right or left hand on the respective stereo channel. This allows you to play along with all pieces requiring both hands by listening to one hand on the CD and playing the other.

The wide spectrum of musical styles presented here opens up the path to the multi-facetted world of accordion playing.

Every track on the CD starts with a so-called count-in click. This enables you to find the beginning of an exercise or song more easily.

Have fun and much success with *Accordion Basics*!


Herb Kraus

# Table of contents

Preface . . . . . . . . . . . . . . . . . . . . . . . . . . . . . . . . . . . . . . . . . . . . . . . . 3

1.  How to practice properly . . . . . . . . . . . . . . . . . . . . . . . . 6

2.  The notes . . . . . . . . . . . . . . . . . . . . . . . . . . . . . . . . . . . . 7

3.  The note values . . . . . . . . . . . . . . . . . . . . . . . . . . . . . . . 8

4.  Time signature . . . . . . . . . . . . . . . . . . . . . . . . . . . . . . . . 8

5.  Counting the note values . . . . . . . . . . . . . . . . . . . . . . . . 9

6.  Measure and bar line . . . . . . . . . . . . . . . . . . . . . . . . . . . 9

7.  The right-hand keys . . . . . . . . . . . . . . . . . . . . . . . . . . . 10

8.  How to hold the accordion . . . . . . . . . . . . . . . . . . . . . . 12

9.  Whole note exercises . . . . . . . . . . . . . . . . . . . . . . . . . . 15

10.  Half note exercises . . . . . . . . . . . . . . . . . . . . . . . . . . . 17

11.  Quarter note and whole note exercises . . . . . . . . . . . . 19

12.  Quarter note and half note exercises . . . . . . . . . . . . . 20

13.  Ode to joy . . . . . . . . . . . . . . . . . . . . . . . . . . . . . . . . . 21

14.  Alles neu macht der Mai . . . . . . . . . . . . . . . . . . . . . . . 21

15.  Repeat signs . . . . . . . . . . . . . . . . . . . . . . . . . . . . . . . . 22

16.  Quarter note and eighth note exercises . . . . . . . . . . . . 23

17.  The bass side . . . . . . . . . . . . . . . . . . . . . . . . . . . . . . . 24

18.  Exercise with single bass notes . . . . . . . . . . . . . . . . . . 26

19.  Exercise with bass chords . . . . . . . . . . . . . . . . . . . . . . 27

20.  Exercise with C bass and G bass . . . . . . . . . . . . . . . . . 28

21.  Playing with both hands . . . . . . . . . . . . . . . . . . . . . . . 29

22.  Rests . . . . . . . . . . . . . . . . . . . . . . . . . . . . . . . . . . . . . . 31

23.  ¾ time . . . . . . . . . . . . . . . . . . . . . . . . . . . . . . . . . . . . 33

24.  Oh, wie wohl . . . . . . . . . . . . . . . . . . . . . . . . . . . . . . . 35

25.  Kuckuck . . . . . . . . . . . . . . . . . . . . . . . . . . . . . . . . . . . 35

26.  The major scale . . . . . . . . . . . . . . . . . . . . . . . . . . . . . 36

27. Crossing under and crossing over . . . . . . . . . . . . . . . . . . . . . . . 37

28. Fuchs, du hast die Gans gestohlen . . . . . . . . . . . . . . . . . . . . . . 39

29. Accidentals . . . . . . . . . . . . . . . . . . . . . . . . . . . . . . . . . . . . 40

30. All tones within one octave . . . . . . . . . . . . . . . . . . . . . . . . . . 41

31. G major . . . . . . . . . . . . . . . . . . . . . . . . . . . . . . . . . . . . . . 42

32. Bald gras ich am Neckar . . . . . . . . . . . . . . . . . . . . . . . . . . . . 43

33. Die Tiroler sind lustig . . . . . . . . . . . . . . . . . . . . . . . . . . . . . . 44

34. Midnight Special . . . . . . . . . . . . . . . . . . . . . . . . . . . . . . . . . 45

35. The dotted quarte note . . . . . . . . . . . . . . . . . . . . . . . . . . . . . 46

36. Wenn ich ein Vöglein wär' . . . . . . . . . . . . . . . . . . . . . . . . . . . 46

37. The tie . . . . . . . . . . . . . . . . . . . . . . . . . . . . . . . . . . . . . . . 47

38. Trink den herrlichen Wein . . . . . . . . . . . . . . . . . . . . . . . . . . . 48

39. F major . . . . . . . . . . . . . . . . . . . . . . . . . . . . . . . . . . . . . . . 49

40. Lang ist's her . . . . . . . . . . . . . . . . . . . . . . . . . . . . . . . . . . . 50

41. Sur le pont d'Avignon . . . . . . . . . . . . . . . . . . . . . . . . . . . . . . 50

42. The minor chords . . . . . . . . . . . . . . . . . . . . . . . . . . . . . . . . . 51

43. When the saints go marching in . . . . . . . . . . . . . . . . . . . . . . . 52

44. The dominant 7th chords . . . . . . . . . . . . . . . . . . . . . . . . . . . . 53

45. Mein Hut, der hat drei Ecken . . . . . . . . . . . . . . . . . . . . . . . . . 54

46. Oh, Susanna . . . . . . . . . . . . . . . . . . . . . . . . . . . . . . . . . . . . 55

47. Preliminary exercise for La Paloma . . . . . . . . . . . . . . . . . . . . . 56

48. La Paloma . . . . . . . . . . . . . . . . . . . . . . . . . . . . . . . . . . . . . 58

Appendix . . . . . . . . . . . . . . . . . . . . . . . . . . . . . . . . . . . . . . . . . 61

CD tracklist . . . . . . . . . . . . . . . . . . . . . . . . . . . . . . . . . . . . . . . 64

# 1.   How to practice properly

- Practice regularly every day.

- Make your practicing time a fixed part of your daily routine.

- Always be concentrated and self-critical while practicing.

- Feel every tone. Every tone is important. Every tone is music.

- While getting familiar with an exercise, always count out loud.

- Make sure to use the correct hand posture.

- Make sure to use the correct key attack with the proper fingering.

- Don't skip any exercises. This course is designed in a way that the exercises are based upon one another.

- Before you practice, listen to the playback CD to become familiar with the exercise.

- Practice the pieces for both hands with each hand individually first. When you master the piece with the single hands, play it with both.

- When you come to a difficult point, don't start from the top but practice the difficult part only. Start with a smaller part of two or three notes, for example. Practice this part as slowly as necessary to be able to play it without mistakes. Slightly increase the tempo and play the part accurately several times. Now add several notes step by step and start again slowly. When you are able to play the entire exercise at a slow tempo, increase the tempo again in small steps up to the target tempo.

- To finally control yourself, play along to the CD.

- It is quite normal that it often takes several days or weeks to master difficult passages.

- Play a piece several times without mistakes before going to the next one.

# 2. The notes

Notes are notated in a **staff**. This system consists of 5 lines. The notes are notated either on or in between the lines. The pitch depends on the line or space where the note is placed. The name of every note is based on this.

The **clef** is notated at the beginning of a staff. It determines what tone corresponds to a note. Both clef and note position determine the name of the note. The right-hand notes of the accordion are notated in the **treble clef**.

The pitch of a note depends on the line or space where the note is placed..

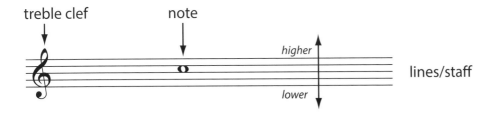

Notes that are too high or low for the staff are notated with the so-called **ledger lines**.

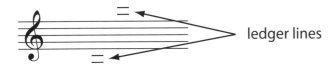

The curl of the **treble clef** spirals around the line on which tone G is notated. For this reason, it is called G clef as well.

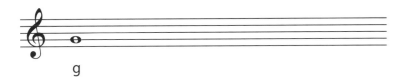

The left-hand notes for the accordions are notated in the **bass clef**. The bass clef is curved and has 2 dots. The two dots are located above and below the line on which the note F is notated. Therefore, it is called **F clef** as well.

# 3.    The note values

The **note values** indicate the time duration of a note or tone.

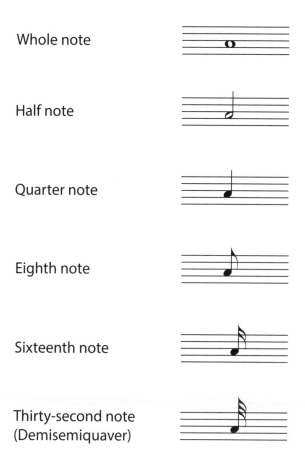

Whole note

Half note

Quarter note

Eighth note

Sixteenth note

Thirty-second note
(Demisemiquaver)

# 4.    Time signature

The **time signature** is indicated behind the clef. It tells us how many notes make up a whole bar.

**Example:** The time signature $^4/_4$ notated behind the clef indicates that 4 quarter notes fit in one measure or as many notes that are individually (the whole note) or as a group equivalent to the value of 4 quarter notes.

4 quarter notes equal a whole note. So, one whole note fills a complete measure in $^4/_4$ time. One half note and two quarter notes also exactly fill a complete measure in $^4/_4$ time. C is often notated instead of the $^4/_4$ time signature as well.

Other time signatures are $^2/_4$, $^3/_4$ or $^6/_8$, for example.

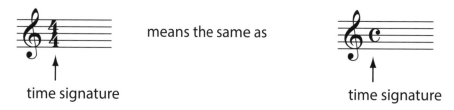

means the same as

time signature                                                    time signature

# 5.   Counting the note values

A whole note has the same time duration as two half notes, four quarter notes, eight eighth notes, sixteen sixteenth notes and so forth.
To make things clearer in the staff, the "flags" of single eighth or sixteenth notes are notated as **beams**, whenever more than one note of the same note value occurs

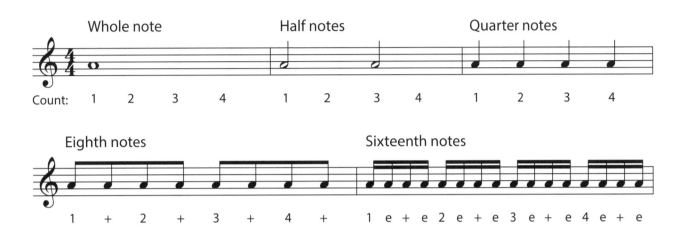

# 6.   Measure and bar line

The vertical lines of the staff are called **bar lines**. They separate the measures from each other. A double bar line indicates a musical section. A double bar line (with the right one thicker than the left) shows the end of a musical piece.

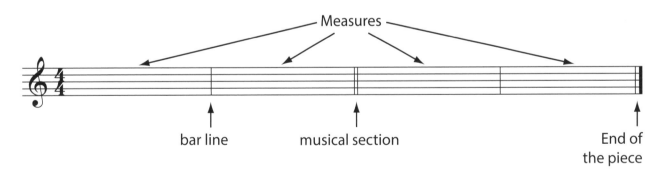

# 7.   The right-hand keys

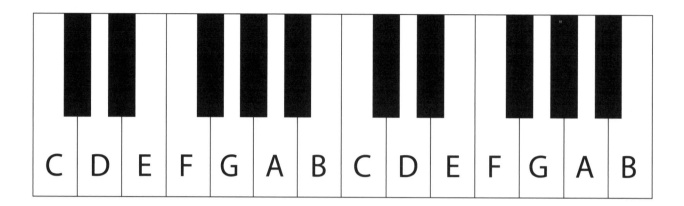

In the graphic above you can clearly recognize one group of **two black keys** and one group of **three black keys** in a repeating pattern.

This layout allows us to name the keys.

Examples:

The note "C" is always located to the **left** of the **two** black keys.
The note "D" is always located **in between** the **two** black keys.
The note "E" is always located to the **right** of the **two** black keys.
The note "F" is always located to the **left** of the **three** black keys.
etc.
The names of the black keys of your piano will be discussed later in this book.

Depending on the configuration and type of an accordion, the right-hand keys do not always start with the tone C, but may as well start with G, for example. In this case, two groups of two black keys follow one after. Then, one of the two groups of three is shorter with the third black key missing (see illustration below).

# 8.    How to hold the accordion

Tighten the shoulder straps so that the accordion is close to the body. The keyboard of the right hand (treble side) is held vertically over the right side of the chest. When opening and closing the bellows, the treble side does not move. The bellows movement is performed exclusively with the left hand.

In the beginning, always sit down when playing. Make sure to keep your back straight. Holding the accordion is supported additionally by resting the instrument on the thighs.
At the top and bottom of the casing, the accordion has bellows straps to hold the bellows closed. Before you start playing, undo the straps to make the bellows playable.
When you are done playing, you should secure the bellows again by closing the straps.

To adjust the (leather) strap for the bellows motion, the accordion usually has a setscrew in its casing on top of the bass buttons side. By means of this screw, the strap can be adjusted so that the left hand can easily reach the bass buttons with the back of your hand touching the strap at the same time.

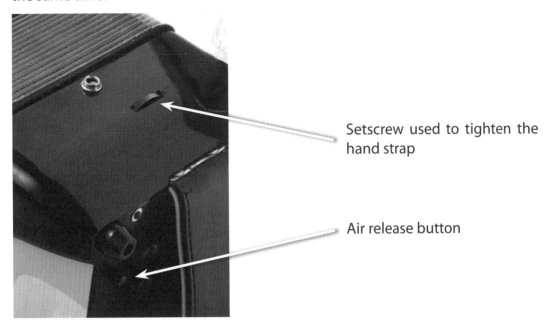

Setscrew used to tighten the hand strap

Air release button

The first exercises are played with the right hand only. The left hand focuses on the opening and closing of the bellows.

Place the thumb of the right hand on the low C. The low C is located at the top end of the instrument, where the low position is located. In the notation, the C in this position is indicated as the **middle C** (C') or C1.

**Low position (low tones)**

**High position (high tones)**

C1

C2

C3

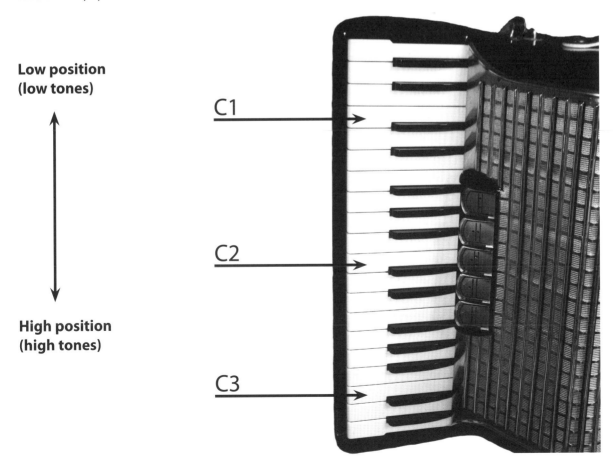

Now place the other right-hand fingers one after the other on the following keys:

| | |
|---|---|
| Index finger on | D |
| Middle finger on | E |
| Ring finger on | F |
| Little finger on | G |

Make sure to keep the fingers slightly rounded.

Strike the tone C (C1) with your thumb. The other fingers stay in their starting position.
Lift the thumb again and repeat this exercise several times.
Strike the tone D with your index finger. Again, the other fingers do not change.
Lift the index finger again and repeat this exercise several times.
Practice this with the middle and ring finger and the pinky as well.
To determine which finger is to play a key, a figure is assigned to every finger. (In this tutorial, the fingering is indicated above the staff.)

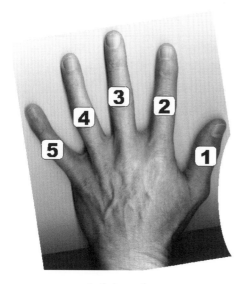

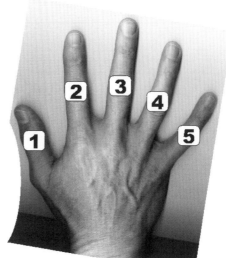

1 = thumb
2 = index finger
3 = middle finger
4 = ring finger
5 = pinky

left hand                    right hand

# 9.   Whole note exercises

Slip your left hand under the hand strap on the bass (button) side. Slide your left hand under the hand strap of the bass (button) side. Push the air release button (see illustration on page 13"). Draw and press the bellows several times slowly and carefully by means of the hand strap.
At the beginning of an exercise, the bellows are always closed.
Play C (C1) with the right-hand thumb and smoothly draw the bellows outwards with the back of your left hand. Count out loud  and evenly 1, 2, 3, 4.
Then play C again, pressing the bellows back together with your left hand. Again, count out loud and evenly 1, 2, 3, 4.

Repeat this exercise several times.

**At the end of an exercise, always press the air release button and close the bellows. This way, every new exercise can start with the drawing motion again.**

This is the symbol used in this book to indicate the **opening of the bellows** (draw) ⌐ .

This is the symbol used in this book to indicate the **closing of the bellows** (press) > .

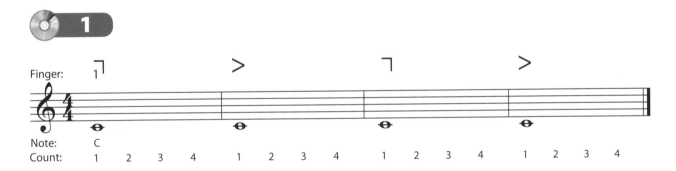

Always count out loud when playing the following exercises.

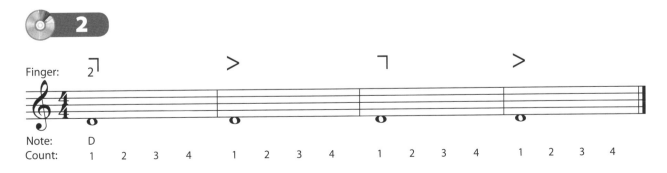

15

**3**

Finger: 3⌐

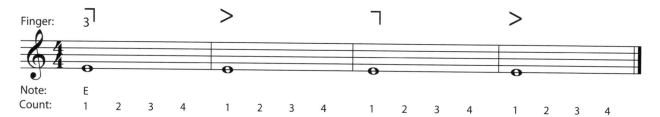

Note: E

Count: 1 2 3 4 1 2 3 4 1 2 3 4 1 2 3 4

**4**

Finger: 4⌐

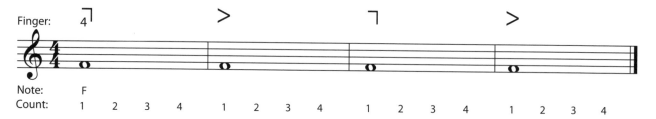

Note: F

Count: 1 2 3 4 1 2 3 4 1 2 3 4 1 2 3 4

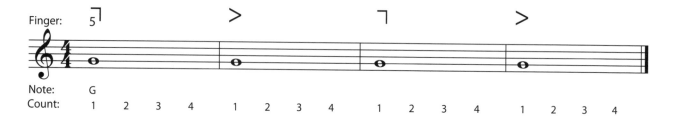

**5**

Finger: 5⌐

Note: G

Count: 1 2 3 4 1 2 3 4 1 2 3 4 1 2 3 4

# 10. Half note exercises

Half notes have hollow note heads and a stem.
A half note has 2 counts, such as 1, 2 or 3, 4.

The stems are notated pointing upwards for all the notes up to the one under the middle line in the staff and downwards for notes from the middle line on.

Start the exercises with the closed bellows again. The exercises (CD tracks 6 to 10) are played by switching from drawing to pressing in every measure.

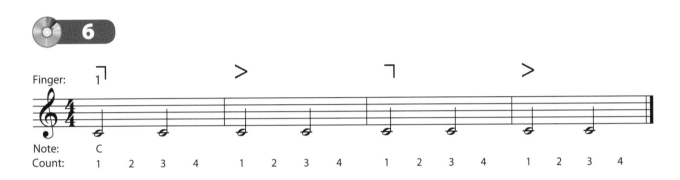

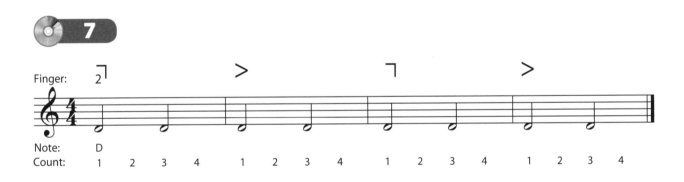

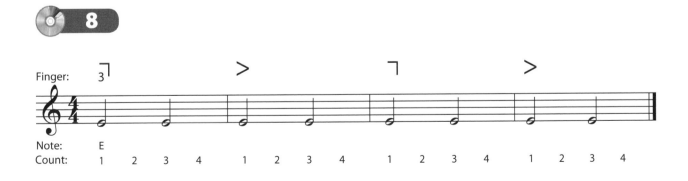

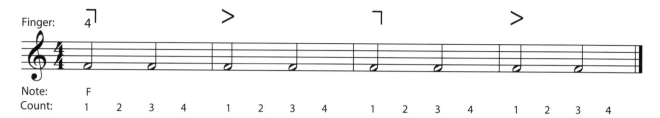

Finger: 4

Note: F

Count: 1 2 3 4 1 2 3 4 1 2 3 4 1 2 3 4

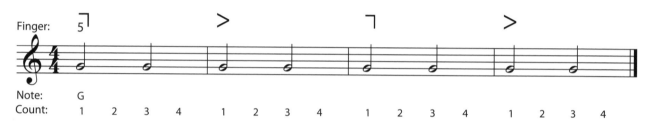

Finger: 5

Note: G

Count: 1 2 3 4 1 2 3 4 1 2 3 4 1 2 3 4

# 11.  Quarter note and whole note exercises

In the following exercise, you play two measures drawing and two pressing the bellows. Move the bellows evenly and slowly. Use the same fingering as in the previous exercises.

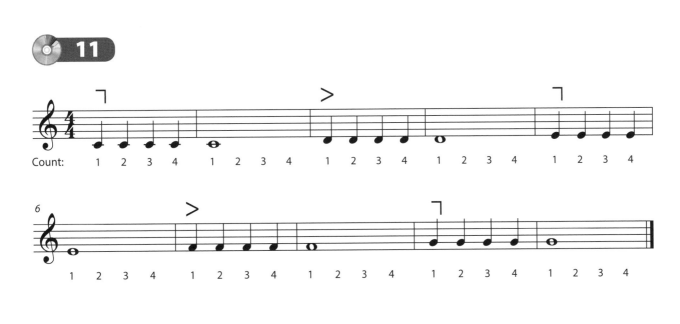

# 12. Quarter note and half note exercises

Count:

Count:

Count:

# 13. Ode to joy

(rhythmically simplified version)

Ludwig van Beethoven

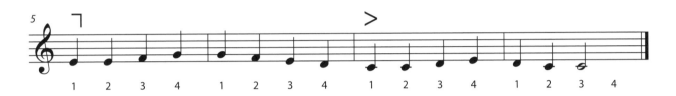

Count: 1 2 3 4 1 2 3 4 1 2 3 4 1 2 3 4

1 2 3 4 1 2 3 4 1 2 3 4 1 2 3 4

# 14. Alles neu macht der Mai

Folk song

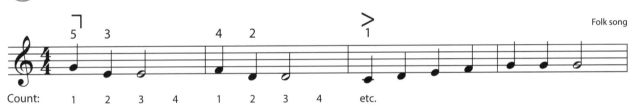

Count: 1 2 3 4 1 2 3 4 etc.

# 15.  Repeat signs

(As the following examples are only about what kind of repeat is used, there are no notes notated in the staff.)

A colon followed by a vertical double line (one thicker than the other) is a repeat sign.

a) If there is no sign notated for the beginning of the repeat, the repeat starts at the beginning of the piece.

The repeat starts at the beginning of the piece:

b) If only a part of the music is to be repeated, this section has a repeat sign at the beginning as well.

Only the measures in between the repeat signs are repeated:

# 16. Quarter note and eighth note exercises

Note the repeat signs.

Count: 1 + 2 3 + 4  1 + 2 3 + 4  1 + 2 3 + 4  1 2 3 4

Count: 1 + 2 + 3 4  1 + 2 + 3 4  1 + 2 + 3 4  1 + 2 + 3 4

Count:

# 17.   The bass side

The bass side is played with the left hand. The buttons on the bass side include single bass tones (low notes) as well as accompanying chords. A chord is the simultaneous sounding of several tones. These tones always have a specific structure which defines the chord type. The chords occur on the accordion in the following order:

**Major triad**
**Minor triad**
**Dominant 7th chord**
**Diminished chord**

(see illustration on the following page)

The bass tones and chords are notated in the bass clef.
A more detailed description is not yet necessary at this point.

The single bass tones are notated with a capital letter and all chords with a small letter, if needed with addition. A minor chord, for example, receives an additional „m".

For orientation reasons, the button for the bass tone C is specially marked, either indented or crosshatched.

**Note:**
The bass tones and chords notated as quarter notes are usually played staccato.

The illustration shows the layout of the bass keys of an accordion with 72 basses. The inner, framed part shows the bass tones of an accordion with 32 basses.

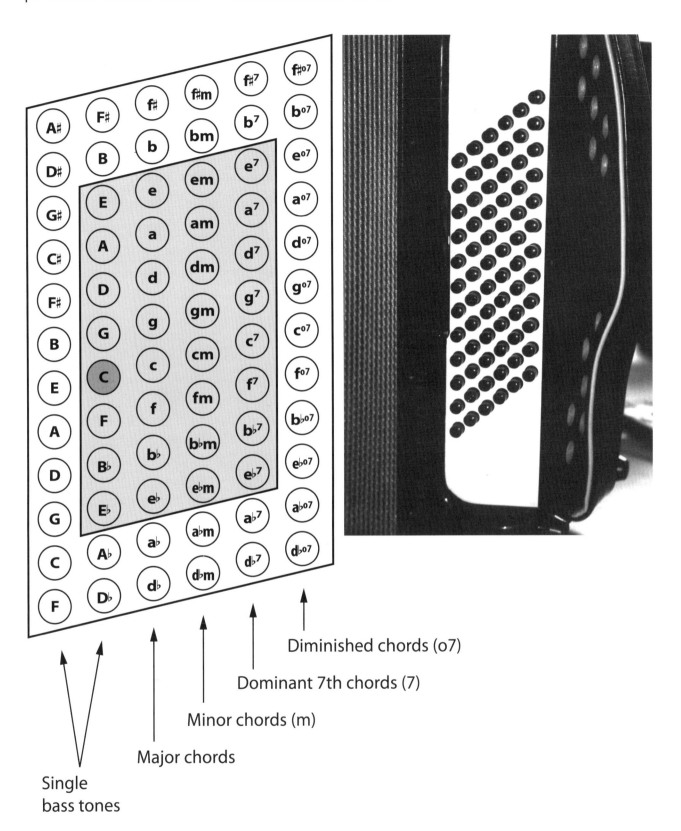

Diminished chords (o7)

Dominant 7th chords (7)

Minor chords (m)

Major chords

Single
bass tones

# 18. Exercise with single bass notes

Place the left-hand **ring finger** on the C bass button.
As mentioned above, the C bass button is specially marked.

Play the bass notes staccato. To be safe, listen to the CD first to check how to play the bass notes.

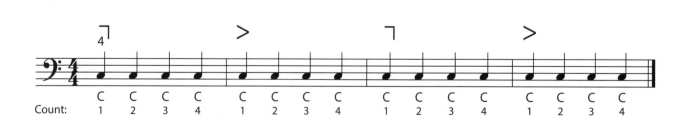

# 19.  Exercise with bass chords

As the bass chords are additionally notated with a small letter, it is not necessary at this point to explain the structure of the chords and their notes in the staff in more detail.

The bass button for the C major chord is located in the same row outwards next to the C bass tone.

The illustration below shows the C area with the neighboring bass tones and chords.

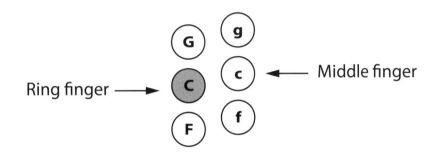

The C major chord is fingered with the middle finger.

Play the chords staccato. To be safe, listen to the CD first to check how to play the chords.

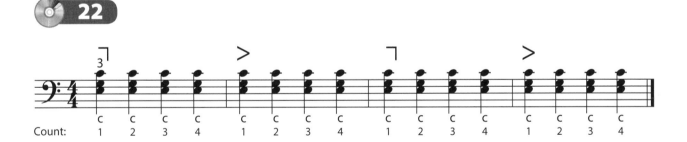

The next exercises combine the bass tones and chords.
Note the repeat signs.

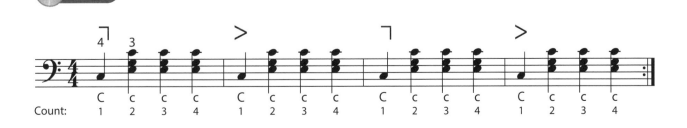

# 20.    Exercise with C bass and G bass

The G bass tone is located right above the C bass tone and is played with the ring finger.

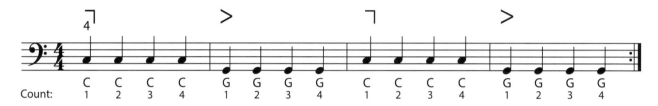

The next exercises combine bass tones and chords again. The G major chord is located right next to the G bass tone (see graphic in chapter 19) and is played with the middle finger.

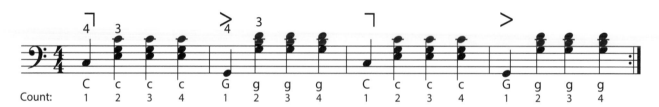

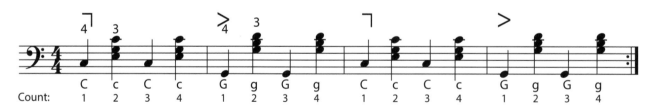

# 21. Playing with both hands

Always practice with each hand individually, then both hands together.

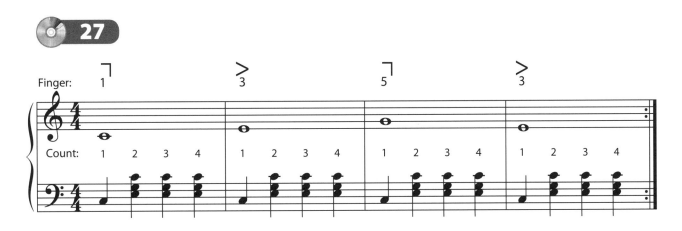

In the last measure of the following exercise, the left hand plays the bass note and the chord at the same time.

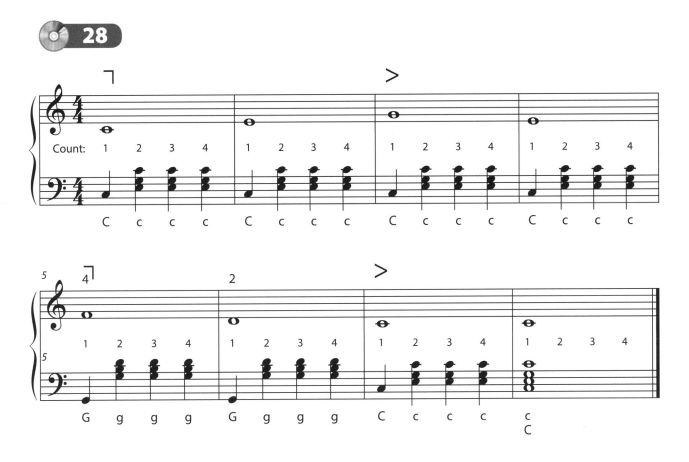

Note the repeat.

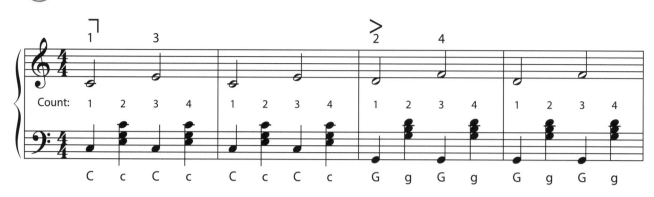

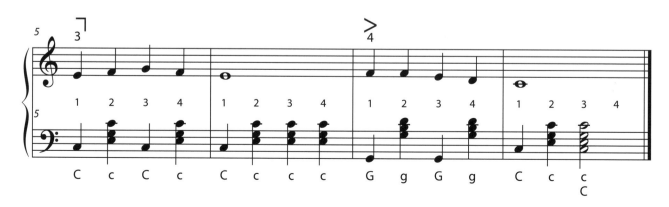

Note that on count 3 in the last measure, the left hand holds the bass tone with the chord for the time duration of a half note.

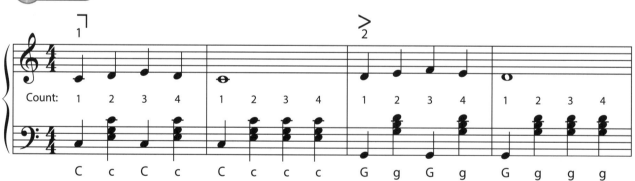

# 22. Rests

Every note value has a corresponding rest. During a rest, no tone is played.
Rests are counted according to their value as it is done with notes.

These are the most common note values and their corresponding rests:

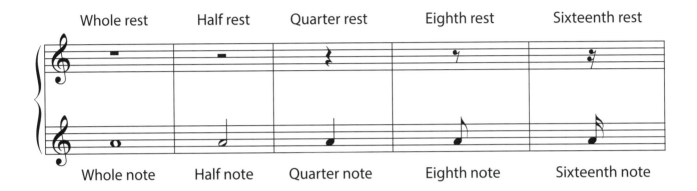

A rest is a good spot to change the bellows direction.

In the following exercises, we no longer indicate any bellows signs. Change the bellows motion either during the rests or at the beginning of a measure. Make sure to keep the melody flowing without interruptions.

**Always begin a song or exercise with a draw.**

Count:    1    2    3    4     1    2    3    4     1    2    3    4     1    2    3    4

1    2    3    4     1    2    3    4     1    2    3    4     1    2    3    4

Practice with each hand individually first, then both hands together. Count out loud.

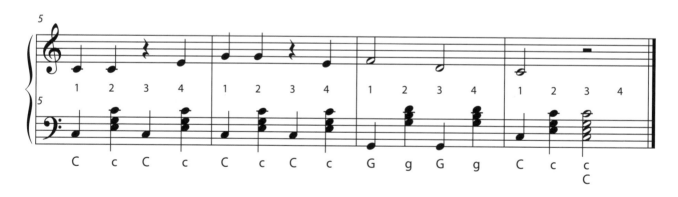

# 23.    ¾ time

In ¾ time, each measure has a duration of 3 quarter notes. So, you have to count three quarter beats per measure: 1, 2, 3.
The waltz dance is always in ¾ time. Therefore, ¾ time is called **waltz** as well.

If a note is to last one complete measure in 3/4 time, it has to have the time duration of three quarter notes.
For this, the half note (= 2 quarter notes) is extended by another quarter note.
This is done by notating a dot directly behind the note.

If a dot is notated behind a note, its value is increased by one-half.
One half note equals 2 quarter notes.
½ divided by 2 is ¼.
Therefore, $^2/_4 + ¼ = ¾$.

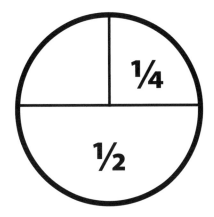

A dotted half note equals three quarter notes.

A dotted half rest equals three quarter rests.

The count-in on the CD for a piece in  ¾ time has three clicks.

Note the dotted half rest before the repeat.

Count:   1   2   3   1   2   3   1   2   3   1   2   3

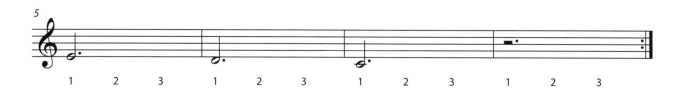

5

1   2   3   1   2   3   1   2   3   1   2   3

Count:   C   c   c   C   c   c   G   g   g   G   g   g
         1   2   3   1   2   3   1   2   3   1   2   3

5

G   g   g   G   g   g   C   c   c   c
                                    C
1   2   3   1   2   3   1   2   3   1   2   3

## 24. Oh, wie wohl

Based on a folk song

## 25. Kuckuck

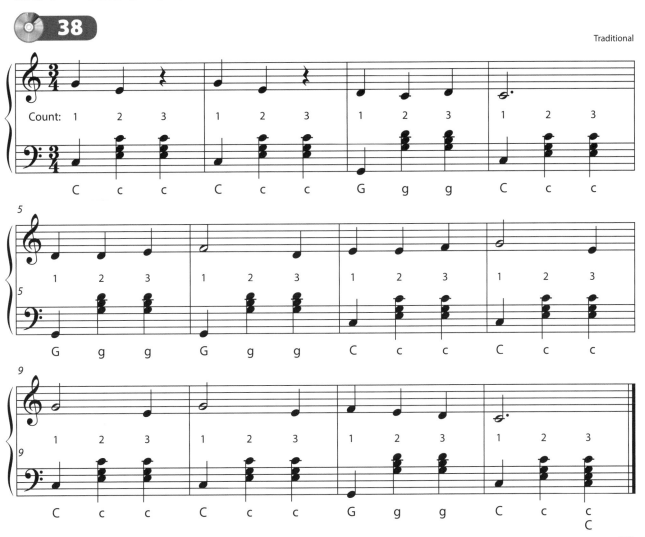

Traditional

# 26.   The major scale

As shown in chapter 7, the keys of the treble side of the accordion (right hand) are arranged in a specific pattern.

The tablature shows different step sizes for certain key (tone) progressions.

There is a (black) key located between tone C and the next tone D. Therefore, the step from C to D is a **whole step**. A black key is also located between D and E, F and G, G and A, A and B. All these steps are whole steps.
There is no key located between E and F. Therefore, the step from E to F is a **half step**. The step from B to C is a half step as well.

So, the half steps in this scale are located between the 3rd and 4th and
the 7th and 8th note. This pattern of whole and half steps forms the **major scale**.

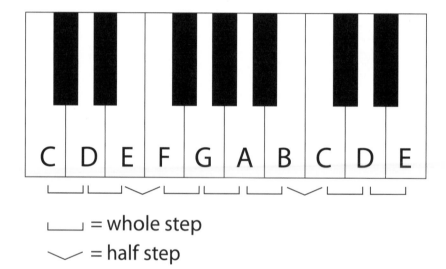

```
[___] = whole step
 \_/  = half step
```

---

**The half steps of the major scale are located between the 3./4. and the 7./8. tone.**

---

The first note of a scale is called the **root**. The root of the C major scale is C.

# 27.  Crossing under and crossing over

This playing technique allows you to smoothly play melody passages that go beyond the five-note range without gaps.

When **ascending** the C major scale, thumb, index finger and middle finger play the first 3 tones C, D and E. Now the thumb crosses under the middle finger to play F. Then the other fingers play G, A, B and C consecutively.

When **descending** the C major scale, the pinky, ring finger, middle finger, index finger and thumb consecutively play the tones C, B, A, G, F.
Then the middle finger crosses over the thumb to play E and the index finger and thumb are in the position to play D and C again.

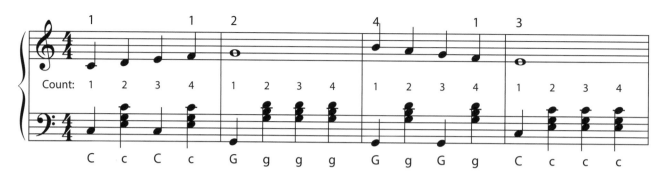

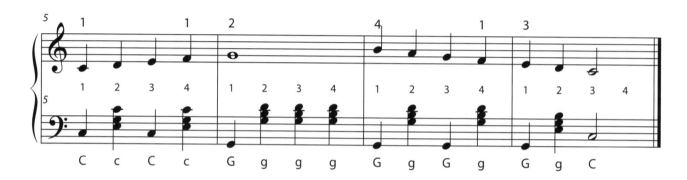

In the following exercise, the left hand always plays the bass note and chord simultaneously.
Make sure to play all bass notes staccato.
Practice with the hands individually first and then both hands together.
Count out loud.

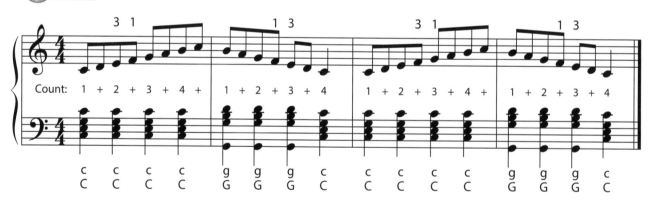

# 28.  Fuchs, du hast die Gans gestohlen

The next piece presents a new bass note and chord: F and F major.
The F bass note is right below the C bass note. The F major chord is located right below the C major chord as well (see illustration).

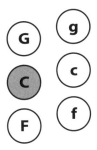

Practice with each hand individually first. When you master playing the single hands without mistakes, play with both together.

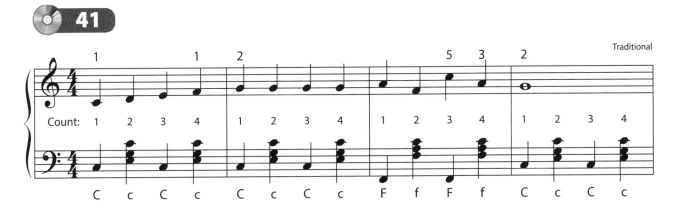

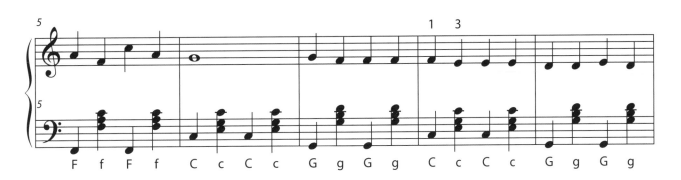

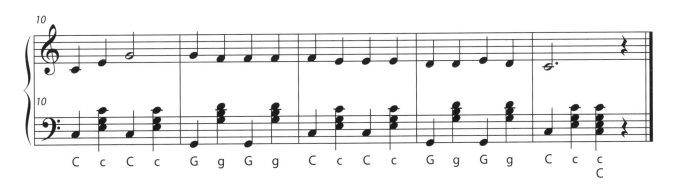

# 29. Accidentals

There are three different kinds of accidentals:

1. The sharp (♯) **raises** the pitch by a half step.
   Example: F♯ (f sharp)

2. The flat (♭) **lowers** the pitch by a half step.
   Example: B♭ (b flat)

The international name of the German H is B.
The international name of the German B is B flat.

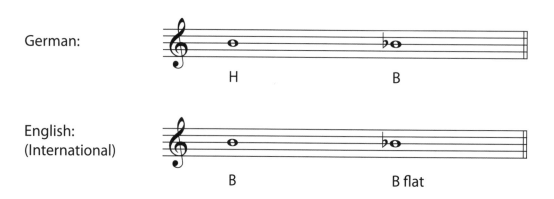

German:

H             B

English:
(International)

B             B flat

3. A natural (♮) **cancels** all accidentals and restores a note to its normal position.

A special form of sharp is the double sharp (𝄪). It raises a given note by two half steps. It is common to notate the sounding tone, which means G for example, instead of an F with a double sharp.

A special form of flat is the double flat (♭♭). It lowers a given note by two half steps. It is common to notate the sounding tone, which means A for example, instead of a B with a double flat.

An accidental placed at the beginning of a musical piece applies to the entire piece and all notes of the same name, no matter in what position these are notated.
An accidental that is placed immediately in front of a note only applies to the following notes of the same name in the given measure. It does no longer apply in the next measure.

Example:

F♯   F    F   F   F♯   F♯   F♯   F   F♯   F♯    F   F   F♯   F♯

Note in the example above that the tone on the first count in the third measure is called F sharp, because the accidental notated at the beginning of the piece still applies.

# 30.  All tones within one octave

The following keyboard shows that the same black keys have different names, such as D♯ (sharp) or E♭ (flat). This is basically the identical tone.

The difference between the two is whether you start on D and raise the tone or on E and lower it. When one and the same note has two different names, we call this **enharmonic equivalent**.

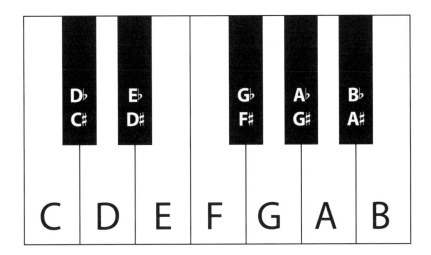

# 31.  G major

The key G major starts on the root note g. The half and whole step pattern of a major scale starts on the root note G now.

When ascending on the white keys starting on G, the 3. step is B and the 4. is C. As it is a half step from B to C, the first condition for a major scale is met.
Continue ascending and you will see that going from the 6. tone (E) to the 7. tone (F) is a half step.
Then we have a whole step in between the 7. tone (F) and the 8. tone (G).
These two do **not** correspond with the major scale definition. Therefore, we raise the tone F to F♯ (sharp), which creates the half step between the 7. and 8. tone and at the same time the whole step between the 6. and the 7. tone.
Now, the definition of the major scale is fulfilled and we have created the G major scale.

**Note**: The structure of the major scales and the corresponding sequence is explained in the appendix under „Circle of Fifths".

The G major scale:

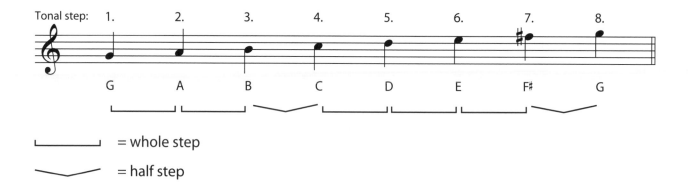

Scale exercises:

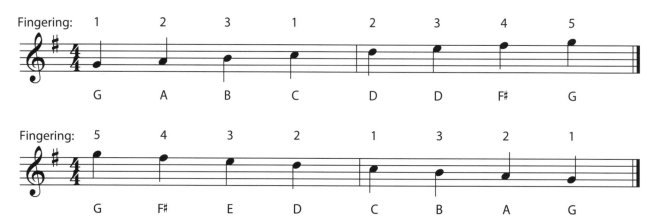

# 32.  Bald gras ich am Neckar

A new bass tone respectively chord is presented in the next piece: D respectively D major. The D bass tone is located immediately above the G bass tone. Also, the D major chord is located immediately above the G major chord (see illustration).

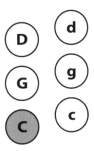

This piece starts with a so-called **pick-up measure**. A pick-up measure is an incomplete measure starting before the first full measure. Pick-up and final measure make a whole measure again.
The count-in on the example CD has 5 clicks. The counts are 1, 2, 3, 1, 2. The song then starts on a pick-up measure on 3.
The piece ends after the repeat on **Fine** in the last measure.

Practice each hand individually first, then both hands together.

# 33.   Die Tiroler sind lustig

Note the fingering in the third to last measure on count 3. The middle finger moves to the tone A here. In the following measure, the F♯ on counts 2 and 3 is played with the 2. finger. The final tone G is played with the 1. finger.
The count-in click is counted 1, 2, 3, 1, 2.
Then the piece starts with the pick-up measure on count 3.

The piece ends after the repeat on **Fine** in the last measure.

Practice with each hand individually, then both hands together.

Folk song

# 34. Midnight Special

This piece starts with a pick-up measure on count 2. The count-in on the example CD has 5 clicks. The counts are 1, 2, 3, 4, 1. Then the song starts with the pick-up measure on count 2.

Practice with each hand individually, then with both hands together.

American folk song

# 35.   The dotted quarte note

As described in chapter 23, a dot written behind a note increases its value by one-half. This means, a dotted quarter note has the time duration of a quarter note plus an eighth note. If a dotted quarter note starts on count 1, the following note is on count 2+.

Example 1:

Count:        1      2    +    3     4          1      2    +    3     4

Example 2:

Count:        1       2    +    3           1       2    +    3

# 36.   Wenn ich ein Vöglein wär'

Folk song

46

# 37.   The tie

As shown in the above example, the dotted quarter note has the time duration of 1 quarter note + 1 eighth note.

The same can be notated by means of a quarter note that is tied to an eighth note. When two notes are connected by a **tie**, the time duration of the first one is extended by the duration of the second of the same name.

The second note is not played, but the preceding one is played and held for the time duration of the second note.

When using a tie to extend a note, this may extend the time duration even across a bar line.

Count:   1    2    3    4    1    2    3    4    1    2    3    4    1    2    3    4

In the following exercise, the note durations are extended on the eighth note on count 4+. This places an accent on the weak count +.
An accent placed on a weak count is called **syncopation**.

**46**

# 38.  Trink den herrlichen Wein

Practice with each hand individually first, and then both hands together.

Folk song from the Ahr valley

# 39.  F major

F major starts on the root note F. The half and whole step pattern of a major scale starts on the root note F now.

When ascending on the white keys starting on F, the 3. step is A and the 4. is B.

As it is a whole step from A to B, B is lowered to B♭. Now we have a half step between the 3. and 4. tone. Continue ascending on the white keys (C, D, E, F) and you will see that all remaining whole and half steps correspond to the major scale pattern.

The F major scale:

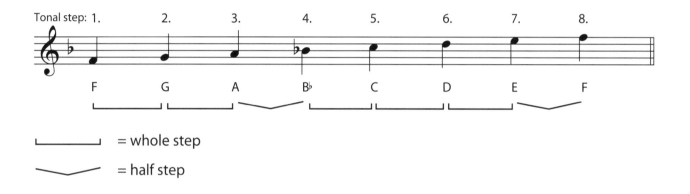

Scale exercises:

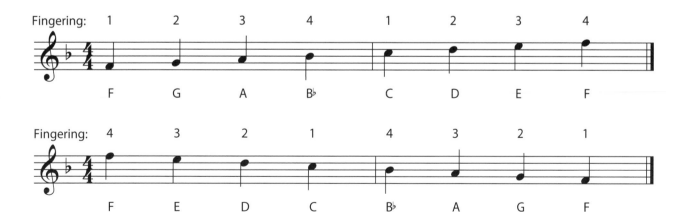

# 40.  Lang ist's her

Practice with each hand individually first, and then both hands together. Note the fingering.

Based on a folk song

# 41.  Sur le pont d'Avignon

Practice with each hand individually first, and then the two hands together.

Folk song from France

# 42.  The minor chords

The button row of the minor chords (m) is located right next to the major chord row.
The minor chord buttons are fingered with the index finger (2. finger).

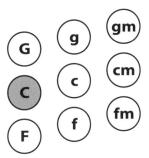

 **50**

 **51**

 **52**

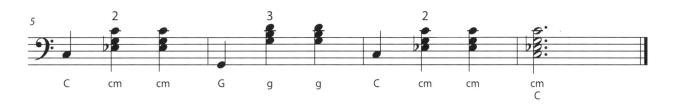

# 43.    When the saints go marching in

This song starts with a pick-up measure on count 2.
The count-in on the CD has 5 clicks: 1, 2, 3, 4, 1. Then the piece starts with the pick-up measure.
Practice with each hand individually first, and then both hands together.

Traditional

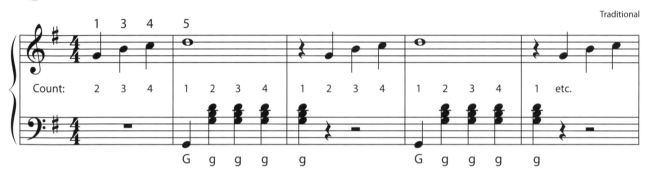

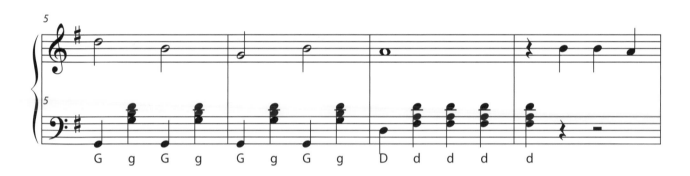

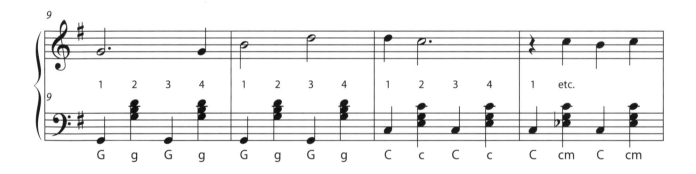

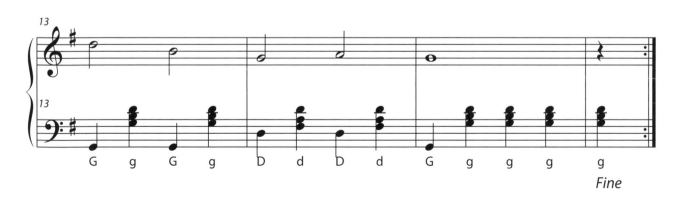

*Fine*

# 44.   The dominant 7th chords

The dominant 7th chords (7) are located on the outward row next to the minor chord row. The dominant 7th chords are fingered with the index finger (2. finger).

A dominant 7th chord is a major chord with an additional flat seven (= 7th tone of the scale). Some smaller squeezeboxes do not have any dominant seventh chords. If this is the case, play the major chord instead..

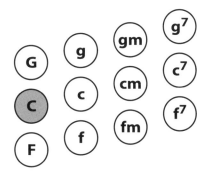

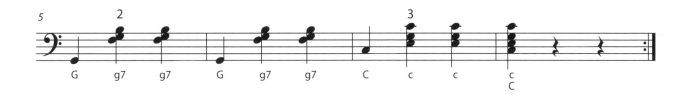

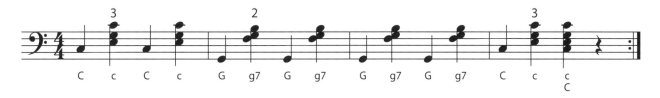

# 45. Mein Hut, der hat drei Ecken

Note the fingering. The count-in has 5 clicks: 1, 2, 3, 1, 2.
The piece starts with a pick-up measure on count 3.

56

Based on a folk song

# 46.  Oh, Susanna

The dominant seventh chord D7 is located right next to the D minor chord (see illustration) and is played with the index finger (2). Practice with each hand individually first and then the two hands together. Note the fingering. The count-in has 7 clicks: 1, 2, 3, 4, 1, 2, 3. The piece then starts with the pick-up measure on count 4.

# 47. Preliminary exercise for La Paloma

The song *La Paloma* is from South America and is one of the most-played musical pieces on the accordion.

The syncopated rhythm in the melody is typical of the style of this music, with its changes from accented to non-accented counts. The eighth notes are commonly phrased in a more laid-back manner.
Repeat the following rhythm exercises until you can play these well.
Listen to the examples on the CD to check how you are doing.

62

Count: 1 + 2 + 3 4  1 + 2 + 3 4  1 + 2 + 3 4  1 2 3 4

63

Count: 1 + 2 + 3 + 4 +  1 2 3 4  1 + 2 + 3 + 4 +  1 2 + 3 4

64

Count: 1 + 2 + 3 + 4 +  1 + 2 + 3 + 4  1 2 3 4

65

Count: 1 2 + 3 4  1 + 2 + 3 4  1 2 + 3 4  1 + 2 + 3 4

# 48. La Paloma

First practice the right hand only. Note the fingering.

Play the piece until you get to the repeat sign of the bracketed 1. ending = [1.        ].
Repeat from the repeat sign at the beginning (measure 5) and do not play the notes of the first ending, but continue with the bracketed 2. ending.
Do the same with the repeats respectively the bracketed endings at the end of the piece.

Based on a folk song

58

# Appendix

## Circle of fifths

The circle of fifths allows us to show various harmonic relations, such as the ones concerning the major scales.

Let's first find out how the circle of fifths is formed.

When looking at the C major scale from C to the next C, you will notice that the scale can be split into two identical halves with 4 tones each, which means 2 whole steps followed by a half step.

Already in ancient Greece, these four tone sequences were called **tetrachords** (tetra = 4)

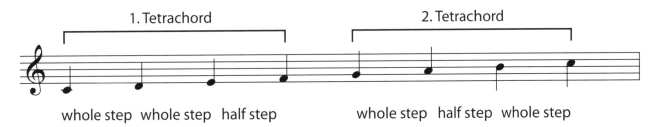

The second tetrachord starts on the scale's fifth tone. As the two tetrachords have the same structure, it seems natural to build a new scale on the first tone of the 2. tetrachord. So, the 2. tetrachord becomes the new 1. tetrachord. The tone sequence is extended step by step upwards with the tone material of the existing C major scale.

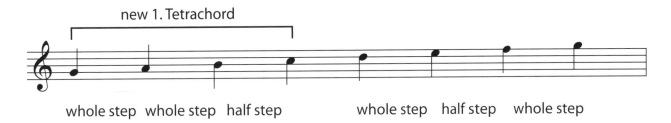

Again, the first 4 tones (1. tetrachord) have the following structure:

whole step - whole step - half step.

However, the following tones have the structure

whole step – half  step – whole step

To maintain the correct structure for the last four notes as well, the note F is raised to F♯.

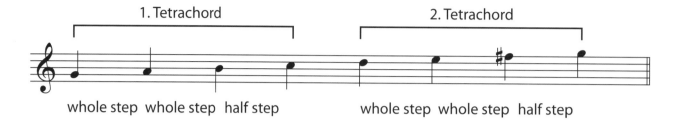

This way, more scales can be formed on the fifth degree of the 2. tetrachord. The 7. note of each new scale is raised by a sharp every time.
If you apply this scale-forming principle to all 12 scales, the final keys receive a very high number of sharps, which makes the whole thing seem rather confusing.

For this reason the principle is looked at from a reverse angle, which means the first four notes of the C major scale are to be analyzed as the 2. tetrachord.

Again, we take the note material of the C major scale and place four notes step by step below the C.

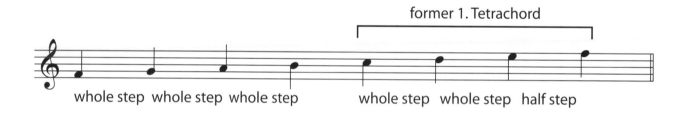

Now the first group of four consists of three whole steps.

To receive the structure of the major scale again, the 4. note (B) is lowered to B♭.

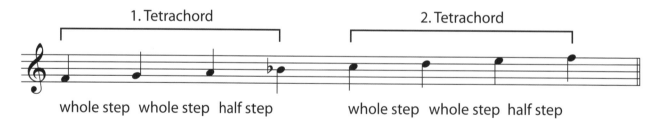

By lowering the 4. note in the first tetrachord of the scale, we receive the major scales of the B keys.

The **circle of fifths** is used to systematically display the keys in a diagram.

## The circle of fifths with the major keys

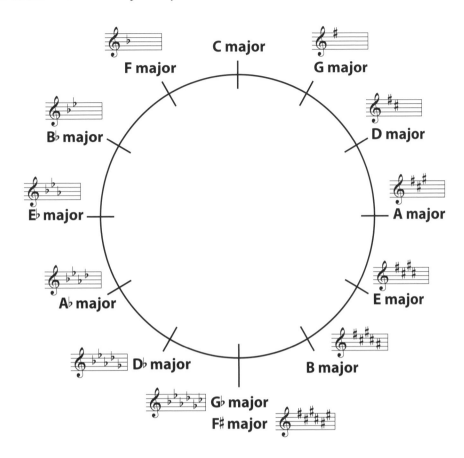

## The circle of fifths with the major keys and their relative minor keys.

The root notes of the relative minor keys are 3 half steps below the relative major key. Both use the same accidentals.

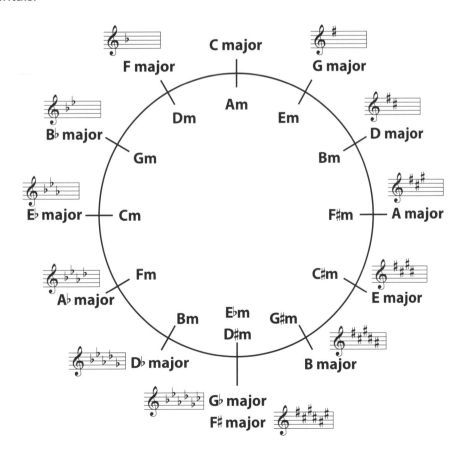

# CD tracklist

| CD track | page | CD track | page |
|---|---|---|---|
| 1 | 15 | 35 | 34 |
| 2 | 15 | 36 | 34 |
| 3 | 16 | 37 Oh, wie wohl | 35 |
| 4 | 16 | 38 Kuckuck | 35 |
| 5 | 16 | 39 | 38 |
| 6 | 17 | 40 | 38 |
| 7 | 17 | 41 Fuchs, du hast die Gans gestohlen | 39 |
| 8 | 17 | 42 Bald gras ich am Neckar | 43 |
| 9 | 18 | 43 Die Tiroler sind lustig | 44 |
| 10 | 18 | 44 Midnight special | 45 |
| 11 | 19 | 45 Wenn ich ein Vöglein wär' | 46 |
| 12 | 19 | 46 | 47 |
| 13 | 20 | 47 Trink den herrlichen Wein | 48 |
| 14 | 20 | 48 Lang ist's her | 50 |
| 15 | 20 | 49 Sur le pont d'Avignon | 50 |
| 16 Ode to joy | 21 | 50 | 51 |
| 17 Alles neu macht der Mai | 21 | 51 | 51 |
| 18 | 23 | 52 | 51 |
| 19 | 23 | 53 | 51 |
| 20 | 23 | 53 When the saints go marching in | 52 |
| 21 | 26 | 54 | 53 |
| 22 | 27 | 55 | 53 |
| 23 | 27 | 56 Mein Hut, der hat drei Ecken | 54 |
| 24 | 28 | 57 Oh, Susanna | 55 |
| 25 | 28 | 58 | 56 |
| 26 | 28 | 59 | 56 |
| 27 | 29 | 60 | 56 |
| 28 | 29 | 61 | 56 |
| 29 | 30 | 62 | 57 |
| 30 | 30 | 63 | 57 |
| 31 | 31 | 64 | 57 |
| 32 | 31 | 65 | 57 |
| 33 | 32 | 66 La Paloma | 58 |
| 34 | 32 | | |